NOTES *from* EDITOR

Well SUMMER Is here and she has come in with grand entrance! The temp has been up in the mid 80s and higher everyday! So, I'm praying that you are drinking plenty of fluids and staying cool!

This Summer edition of the MizCEO Entrepreneurial Magazine was designed with you in mind. This edition is made up of great content on how you can stay Healthy & Fab and make money while doing it!
Healthy is definitely WEALTHY!

We're bringing something new to the MizCEO Entrepreneurial Magazine and that's the MisterCEO Of the Month! And our first pick was the incredibly-intelligent Mr.Jamie McGrone!

He's an Author teaching people "How to Live Their Most Amazing Life"!
One thing these last couple of months have taught me is that you are to take no-one and nothing for granted whom you have in your life! If you love someone-ACT LIKE IT! If you love someone-TELL THEM!

May Everything You Set Your Hands to Do PROSPER!

Because He Lives,

Jessica L. Mosley

Jessica L. Mosley

CONTRIBUTORS

CONTRIBUTING
-WRITERS-

SHANICK BARTELL

JACQUELINE MILLER

DELISA WILLIAMS

CHERYL PEAVY

LASHEERA LEE

SHIRLONDA TAYLOR

SANTISHA WALKER, RN

DR. LESLIE HODGE

DR. DEENA BROWN

WHAT'S INSIDE

TABLE OF CONTENTS

Page 5 ....Meet Angel Richards by Cheryl Peavy

Page 7 ....The Phenomenal Deena Brown

Page 9 ....Blossoming with Santisha Walker

Page 11 ....Introducing Lilie Mae, Owner of Glambitious IAm

Page 12 ....Bershan Shaw-The Unstoppable Warrior Woman

Page 15 ....Cover Story - Vanessa Rogers is Helping Everyone GET and STAY HEALTHY

Page 17 ....Nakita Whittaker by Jacqueline Miller

Page 18 ....Credit is King by Shirlonda Taylor

Page 19 ....It's Always about Potential by Dr.Leslie Hodge

Page 21 ....Health & Wellness-Meet Renee Watts by Santisha Walker

Page 24 ....Black Girls Hear by MizCEO Staff

Page 28 ....MisterCEO of the Month Jamie McGrone

Page 29 ....Why is everyone raving about Delisa Newwilliams?

Page 31 ....Health & Wellness Matters: Women Making It Happen

Page 33 ....MizCEO Feature Of The Month: Nicole Mason

Page 36 ....Cover Story - The Incredible Cheryl Peavy

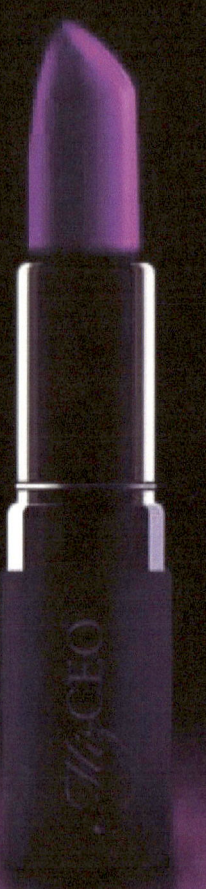

MEET ANGEL RICHARDS

Don't wait until your life is "perfect" to start. People who need help aren't looking for perfection, they are looking for progression.

MEET ANGEL RICHARDS

By Cheryl Peavy

CP: Who is Angel at her core?
AR: When I look past the titles of mother, teacher, author, speaker, life coach, Christian…at my core I am just a woman who's passionate about happiness. I was miserable for so many years of my life and now that I choose happiness- I can't imagine anything else. Although I have bad days that steal my attention, I don't allow them to steal my joy. Being happy is the best feeling and seeing others happy makes me happy. I believe that in that state our world is in right now- personal happiness needs to become a priority. We all have reasons to be unhappy but what reasons do you have to be happy. Focus on that.

CP: Tell us about Clutter Free Society?
AR: Clutter Free Society is an online classroom and community for women who have decided that settling, suffering and staying stuck is no longer an option. Through empowerment sessions, masterclasses, coaching calls and live events, the ladies receive the inspiration and insight needed to create breakthroughs and transform their lives. It serves as a safe place where you can share your truth and be yourself- all while receiving the encouragement and support you need to thrive.

CP: How do you handle setbacks?
AR: With chai tea lattes! Just kidding. I handle all setbacks with clarity. Clarity around why I am experiencing the setback. When you understand why something is happening, you can identify your role (if any) and play a new part next time. Also, clarity about the lesson I could learn from it. I don't believe in failures but in lessons. When you seek out the lesson in any given situation, you open yourself up to growth in that area be it life, love or work.

CP: Where do you see yourself in the next 2-5 yrs?
AR: Coaching couples and families through the process

of decluttering their lives individually and as a unit. My years as a classroom teacher has exposed me to brokenness in the home and how it affects children's confidence, work ethic and dreams. I want to provide the tools needed for couples and families to work through their challenges quickly and effectively so love, peace, and happiness is restored.

CP: What advice do you give women about becoming Clutter Free?
AR: Trust the process. Everyone's clutter free journey is different so you must stay focused on your path and trust that everything you experience along the way is for YOU. The highs and lows, clarity and confusion, love and hate, support and sabotage, excitement and exhaustion... all necessary to prepare you for your next level. This is how we become wiser, stronger and more powerful as women.

CP: What was the biggest obstacle you faced in your business?
AR: Ironically, my biggest obstacle was going full time in my business. I taught elementary school for 13 years and absolutely loved it. However, I knew my season in the classroom was up and I was called to do this work on a larger scale so I retired. This was a dream come true but I started to feel depressed. I no longer had 40+ kids depending on me, parents thanking me, teachers looking to me for leadership, recognition from the administration, a steady paycheck, a strict schedule...I felt lost. It was just ME. I had been helping my clients change their lives for years but my mindset hadn't made the shift from employee to entrepreneur. Fortunately, I was able to breakthrough that block before it started to impact my business or my self-esteem. That was definitely a tough transition for me.

CP: What keeps you motivated to continue to help women?
AR: Their transformations. When you have clients who end toxic relationships and discover their worth or clients who restore broken marriages that were on the verge of divorce or clients who are finally getting their degree after 19 years of stagnation or clients who start their own businesses and find success immediate...how could I not be motivated!

CP: How did you get into your business?
AR: After ending an abusive relationship, I hit rock bottom. I was depressed, bitter, and broken. In fact, it was the only time in my life I felt suicidal. It as bad. But I had what I call- a moment of clarity. There was a moment when I was sitting on the bathroom floor, crying my eyes out, begging God to help me, and I realized I AM THE SOLUTION. I need to make better decisions. I need to work on my issues. I need to heal from my past. I need to forgive myself and others. I need to create my own breakthrough. And I did. I got up and fixed my life- one day, one decision and one prayer at a time. After going through my own transformation, I knew that I wasn't alone and could help others breakthrough too. Hence, the birth of Helping Others Transform, LLC.

CP: What is your key to success?
AR: Commitment. As a two-time teen parent, single mom of 4, who has dealt with abuse, abandonment, divorce, depression- to name a few- it's my NON-NEGOTIABLE commitment to my peace, happiness, and success that has created the life I love today. It's actually our mantra in Clutter Free Society. "My peace, happiness and success are non-negotiable." So when I see something or someone getting in the way of me having success in my relationship, business, or life in general- I'm always willing to let go. You have to be committed to your commitments if you want to manifest and maintain success in any area of your life.

CP: What advice would you give to someone who wants to become a life coach?
AR: Don't wait until your life is "perfect" to start. People who need help aren't looking for perfection, they are looking for progression. They want to know that you can help them progress through their challenges and help them reach their goals. Another tip- don't compare or compete. Every life coach is unique and it's the uniqueness that aligns you with your ideal clients. So be yourself, stay in your lane and start serving.

CP: How can others connect with you?
AR: You can connect with me @hotcoaching on Facebook, Instagram, Twitter, Snapchat, and YouTube as well as www.helpingotherstransform.com

The Phenomenal DEENA BROWN

Time to Get REAL!
"What you find-ah
What you feel now
What you know-ah
To be real
What you find, ah
(I think I love you, baby)
What you feel now
(I feel I need you, baby)
What you know-ah
To be real"

"Got to be Real" Cheryl Lynn (Circa 1978)

In 1978 I was six years old and living my best life … so I thought. My mother Ruby Louise used to play what we now call the classics and what I simply describe as GOOD music. Cheryl Lynn's 'Got to be Real', still makes me jump up and dance. When I hear those opening bars my shoulders start to shimmy and my hips start to sway.

Fast Forward to 2018 and there is nothing realer than pursuing my dreams and fueling mypassion. The thought of walking onto the stage with several hundred people in the audiencecauses my shoulders to shimmy and my hips to sway just like those opening bars to CherylLynn's chart topping song.

The day I decided to "Be Real" instead of a bastardized version of myself my life began tochange. When I decided to show up for ME then the universe was destined to follow.

What does it take to be REAL?
RESILIENCE. The greatest gift that you can give

DEENA BROWN

Got to be real!

yourself is to FIGHT for what is RIGHT for you. Choose to believe in yourself enough to fight for your dreams. The ability to bounce back after suffering a loss whether perceived or tangible is resilience. When life knocks the wind from your sails remember that it's the pressure from the wind against the sail that pushes the craft forward. The storms of your life help propel you into the best version of yourself - embrace it. Success in life has a lot to do with your attitude when you make a choice to see every opportunity whether good, bad, or indifferent as an ingredient to your success your life will be smooth sailing.

EFFICACY. Every dream worth dreaming, every desire worth craving, and every goal worth achieving requires sacrifice. The ability to produce a desired result will require some sacrifice albeit time, money, or mindset. The mindset is the toughest battle ground because we can convince ourselves that we can or can't. Your beliefs influence your level of efforts. You subconsciously strive to "be right" in terms of what you believe about yourself. Your attitude ultimately either pushes you forward or discourages you. As the saying goes, your attitude dictates your altitude.

ACTION. *Lights, Camera, Action* it's your life now it is time for YOU to do something! The very first thing you must do is to shift your mindset so you can move in the right direction. Positive attitudes lead you in the right direction. Ask yourself, "are you the star or an extra in the movie that is your life?" Do you allow negative thoughts, bad experiences, or naysayers to script your divine narrative? Has fear got you STUCK? Fear of failure is like being stuck in quicksand.

You're probably not happy with your current situation, but you're too uncomfortable with your options for making meaningful change your life. *We're great at procrastinating and coming up with 100 reasons why we can't move forward, but those are just manifestations of being afraid.* Fear of failure could actually be a fear of several different things. It might be the fear of being judged or criticized. Or it might just be the fear of wasting time on something that we don't think will work out in the end. Unfortunately, fear can prevent you from every really knowing your true capabilities. It's your life. Choose your own vision of success and take ACTION.

LEVERAGE. Take inventory of your relationships, stock of your ventures, and be mindful of your actions. When you align your actions to your purpose it creates a synergy that causes increased manifestation of your dreams. Evaluate your relationships. Think about your friends, family, neighbors, and coworkers. Which of your relationships could use a little fine tuning? Which relationships need a complete overhaul? And which should be dropped? Leverage your relationships, time, and resources to get the maximum value. If it doesn't add value you to you ... Let it GO!

We are all on the same journey although we travel separate paths. I have learned that living an Unapologetically Authentic version of my life has yielded the greatest results. I was tired of existing in the shadows of hurt, disillusionment , and doubt.

So, as I jam to the classic 1978 tune by Cheryl Lynn, I sing along (slightly off key) at the top of my lungs "I Got to be Real!" I learned to love me unconditionally and I encourage you to make the same commitment.

Dr. Deena C. Brown
Speaker.Teacher.Coach
Instagram @DrDeenaSpeaks
Twitter @DrDeenaSpeaks

Blossoming

Life continues to unfold in each moment, whether we want it to or not. When I think of my life's experiences, I compare them to a blossoming flower. Have you ever taken time to watch a flower bloom? More times than not you will not actually witness the blooming process; but rather, you will look up one day and the flower has completely opened. It was all happening right before your eyes at a very slow pace; however, progress was indeed being made.

Life has a way of strategically connecting the dots throughout the blossoming process; and although there are many phases of being stretched, tempered and tested while the line is being drawn from one dot the next, it all comes together like a masterpiece. I've learned to embrace these "in-between phases" along my entrepreneurial journey and allow these moments to mold me so I can continue to blossom in my purpose. These phases have built my character, my veracity, life's muscles and allow me to operate in my truth. Accepting my life for what it is, then choosing to be receptive to making the necessary changes to grow into who I desire to become has been one of my greatest accomplishments! Hindsight is always 20/20, but I believe the key to success is knowing how to use what you have learned and leverage it to catapult you to the best version of yourself.

I operate in the entrepreneurial realm in various capacities and have come to realize that I am at my best in this arena and absolutely in love with entrepreneurship! As Founder & Owner of Walker Group Health & Wellness, a boutique consulting company specializing in corporate education through highly-qualified health & wellness professionals; as Co-Founder of Temple Vitality Foundation, a 501(c)(3) organization that focuses on bringing awareness to mental illness and help transition this population to a state of independence through healthy living; and as Founder of The Nurse Brandnista,

SANTISHA WALKER - BLOSSOMING

I serve as a coach for nurses desiring to move beyond the traditional realm of nursing, build a thriving brand, live out their heart's desires and make their own mark within the nursing profession, I am living the best version of Santisha! I find it amusing that although I have a Bachelor's Degree in Business Administration, and my parents were avid entrepreneurs, I never envisioned myself as a business owner. I knew obtaining a business degree would afford the opportunity to have general business knowledge and use my skills to work for someone else's business; but Santisha as a business owner? No way. I was not interested. However, the unfolding of life has landed me right where I belong, and now as a nurse I have the amazing opportunity to marry my Business Degree, and my Associate and Masters in Nursing Degrees. The structure of my companies is a perfect fit with my nursing knowledge and personality.

In order for me to love entrepreneurship, I had to ensure it made sense and matched my core personality. The two worlds of nursing and business have mixed so well that others frequently ask if I planned to become a Nurse Entrepreneur when I decided to become a nurse. Nursing never crossed my mind until I had an "ah-ha" moment while obtaining my business degree but chose to put it off. Then when my interest shifted to having a more profound impact on the well-being of others after working in the insurance industry for 5 years, I knew I had to pursue nursing. As my life progressed, I simply followed my heart for helping others in the nursing capacity and embraced the notion that timing is everything!

Today I'm afforded the opportunity to continue witnessing my life unfold as a blossoming flower. As Director of Patient Care Services for a home care agency, I have the pleasure of remaining connected to the clinical setting overseeing the quality of care provided by caretakers in patient's homes. As a Nurse Entrepreneur and Certified Wellness Coach, I have the privilege of educating the general public on health & wellness related topics as a contributing writing, a speaker, through radio, television, authorship, podcasts, and publication features; as well as inspire and connect with the hearts and minds of my brilliant fellow nurses to dream big, build their brand, and live their heart's desires. What a beautiful experience entrepreneurship has been!

It has not been easy and has been one of the most thought-provoking times in my life, but so very rewarding. It's like planting a seed, watering it, nurturing the seed and watching it grow, then sitting back and admiring the stunning results. I'm often asked what fuels my drive? My passion to witness others live the best life God intended them to live and achieve their heart's desires. It's that simple. I appreciate the energy of unadulterated joy, positivity and abundance, and I desire as many as possible to live in these moments as much as possible. I have been blessed with a gift of empowering others to achieve their life goals and offer empowerment through practical tips, guidance and reliable resources. You can find out more about my available resources, inspirational products, and my book revealing my transition from insurance to clinical nursing to nurse entrepreneur, entitled "Stethoscope and A DREAM" at www.santishawalker.com. You can connect with me through my website or social media @santishawalkerrn.

INTRODUCING LILLIE MAE

Introducing...Lillie Mae, Owner of Glambitious IAm

MizCEO: How did you get into your business?
Lillie Mae: While studying at UNC Chapel Hill, I acquired internships in the Public Relations departments of Universal-Motown Records andAtlantic Records. These experiences solidified my interest in the PR industry, and once I relocated to Atlanta after college I hit the ground running!

MizCEO: How do you handle stress in your business?
Lillie Mae: Whenever I feel overwhelmed I allow myself time for a brief mental break to meditate, listen to a podcast or read a book. Once I've calmed down, I take the top 2-3 items on my to-do list and focus on that specifically. Often times stress comes from having too much on our to-do list, and we have to reorganize our approach to handling that workload.

MizCEO: What is your biggest hurdle you've overcome since becoming a business owner?
Lillie Mae: When I first started my business, I felt the need to model it after other businesses in the industry. I now fully embrace my own unique professional flare when working with clients and feel very confident doing so.

MizCEO: What is the biggest achievement you've accomplished with your business?
Lillie Mae: Being a full-time entrepreneur for over 7 years is a huge accomplishment to me. Having the capacity to live and thrive off of my own business efforts is something I am extremely proud of.

MizCEO: In your opinion, what is the key to success?
Lillie Mae: Passion is the key to success. When you are passionate about something you will give it your all, never quit and enjoy a sense of fulfillment that is not money-related.

MizCEO: What is the best business tip you can give a prospective person who is looking to merge into your field?
Lillie Mae: I would suggest getting a mentor in the field and working for a reputable PR agency, before starting a PR business. This will allow you truly hone the skills that are necessary to succeed as an entrepreneur in this field.

MizCEO: What is a quote/mantra that motivates you?
Lillie Mae: "God is within her, she cannot fall; (Psalm 46:5)

BERSHAN SHAW - THE UNSTOPPABLE WARRIOR WOMAN

Unsilenced. Unstoppable.

THE Unstoppable Warrior WOMAN

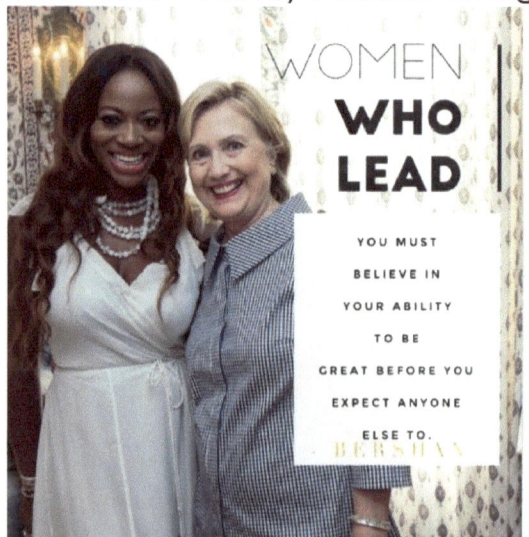

Women are history-makers and groundbreakers. From Cleopatra to Oprah, Mother Theresa to Rosa Parks, Billie Jean King to Malala Yousafazi, women inspire. In 2018, women are breaking more ground than ever in science, politics, sports, entrepreneurship, tech, and entertainment. And, they are finally speaking up and speaking out!

THE UNSTOPPABLE WARRIOR WOMAN movement is a new initiative that empowers women to share their personal narratives, express their experiences, and tell their own stories.

Now, we will un-mute the voices of women all around the world to be heard with their amazing stories of triumph, love, courage, faith strength, and business successes for all to hear to build an unshakable warrior community.

THE UNSTOPPABLE WARRIOR WOMAN movement is spearheaded by the fearless **BERSHAN SHAW**. Shaw is an internationally renowned speaker, author, executive coach, and champion of women. She has dedicated her life to helping others identify their inner warrior and has now created the ultimate platform for women.

THE BOOK: May, 2018

THE UNSTOPPABLE WARRIOR WOMAN book contains honest and inspiring stories from women in all walks of life. From pioneers in tech, law, and finance to soccer moms, retail clerks, and students, this collection of stories offers a new lens on the power women possess and showcases resilience, perseverance, and truth. Some of the stories are tear-jerking, others are laugh out loud hilarious, but the grit and tenacity behind each of them is the backbone for this movement. Through the exchange and celebration of these stories, women everywhere will feel more connected and inspired to do more for themselves and other women around them.

THE CONFERENCES

In collaboration with the book launch, there will be brunches in New York, L.A., and other major cities that feature Bershan and her team of Unstoppable Warrior women. They will come together to speak, share, honor, and build community.

At these gatherings, the movement will take root and attendees will gain tools and confidence so they can return to their own communities to empower the women in their inner circles.

THE COMMUNITY

We know the ripple effect that happens when women band together. Changes are made from the inside in neighborhoods, businesses, pop culture, and public policy. You may not have been born a warrior, but you can become one. Join Bershan and her dynamic, empowered squad in this movement to discover the warrior in you.

> Bershan is teaching women and men all over the world how to stand up inside themselves and live from their truth.
> -Les Brown

This movement is for every man, woman and child to understand that women have stories to teach, share and motivate and it's our time now to share them. I beat my breast cancer diagnosis. I survived my divorce. I am not afraid to tell my story. I am unstoppable. I am a warrior. –Bershan Shaw

**For more information and to join the movement, contact :
Renee Kelly: renee.kelly1@gmail.com and Tiana Robinson: tiana.robinson@gmail.com**

BERSHAN SHAW-THE UNSTOPPABLE WARRIOR WOMAN

"Any time women come together with a collective intention, it's a powerful thing." - Phylicia Rashad

UNSTOPPABLE WARRIOR WOMAN

A COLLECTION OF STORIES FROM SUCCESSFUL WOMEN WHO SURVIVED THE ODDS

CURATED BY BERSHAN SHAW

COVER STORY - VANESSA ROGERS

ON THE MOVE WITH VANESSA ROGERS

By La Sheera Lee

Vanessa Rogers is a woman on a mission.. She is a personal trainer, author, registered nurse, Kangoo Dance, Kangoo Power and Kangoo Jumps Boot Camp Instructor. Whew! Yes, Vanessa Rogers is a woman who is literally and figuratively on the move. She wants to make the world a healthier place through her work and intentional strategies.

Vanessa's own health journey stated when she lost seventy five pounds. She has been able to keep the pounds off for several years. Her journey is not a small feat. According to https://stateofobesity.org/rates/, obesity is on the rise in most states. In fact some states obesity rates have increased by as much as thirty-five percent. Vanessa is not oblivious or insensitive to weight loss headaches. Vanessa understands the struggle and wants to help you look and feel your best. You can find out more about her business and services at www.bouncebackindiana.com

COVER STORY - VANESSA ROGERS

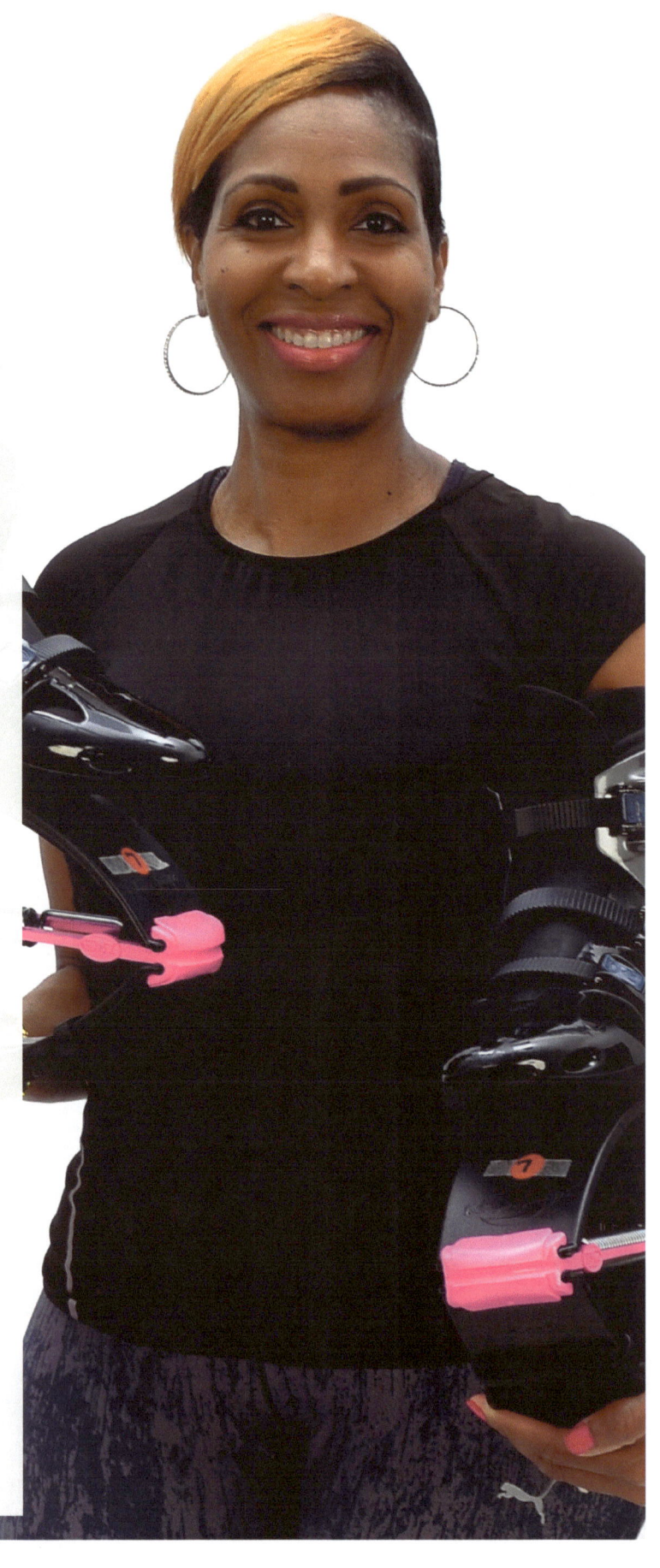

MizCEO Magazine was able to catch up with the dynamic woman of action and learn more about her charge to get us on the right track.

MizCEO Magazine: Vanessa, tell us what you feel is one of the number one factors that prevent people from exercising?
Vanessa: Time management is an important factor in exercising and eating healthy. Most women feel that they don't have time to exercise. However, exercise, in actuality does not take a lot time. In addition, you can schedule activities such as Kangoo Power/Dance,. You can also exercise outdoors or find group fitness activities. Taking a walk or running around your neighborhood, are also good forms of exercises. Select activities that are fun and self motivating. In addition, take time to plan and prep meals in advance. It can be a very healthy and economical strategy for you.

MizCEO: The idea is to trick yourself into believing that exercise is business as usual.
Vanessa: Exercise, of course, has many health components but it can also be fun and a method to engage with family and friends.
Vanessa: At times, some African American Women don't want to exercise because they don't want to mess up their hairstyle. There are protective styles you can wear to assist with that matter.

MizCEO Magazine; Vanessa, I am guilty on that charge.
MizCEO Magazine: Tell me more about Kangoo Jumps Rebound Shoes. I have never heard of it before.
Vanessa: I meet a lot of people who have never encountered the exercise. The exercise use a ski boot like shoe that has a spring on the bottom. In the KJ's you bounce up and

down like you're on a trampoline. The shoe provides up to eighty percent of the impact. Therefore, it is excellent for people with joint issues and the elderly.

MizCEO Magazine: What advice do you have for people on their health journey?
Vanessa: Always consult your physician before you enter into a new exercise or nutrition program. As a certified nutrition coach, I am against fad diets. They can cause a lot of harm. I think you should also set goals. Check them off as you complete them. It will help you keep accountability. Eventually, your goals will become a habit of success.

La Sheera Lee is an award winning blogger, podcaster, moderator, and vision delegate. She loves to help people to see the beauty in their voices. You can catch her on podcast called Read You Later on Blog Talk Radio or iHeart Radio. Follow her on Twitter and Instagram @readyoulater

OVERCOMER. DRIVEN. COMPASSIONATE.

Nakita WHITTAKER

By MizCEO Staff

Survivor are just a few words to describe the phenomenally phenomenal Nakita Whitaker! Life has thrown this heck-of-a –woman some hard challenges! But still, she rises! I had the opportunity to speak with this great, and here is what she had to say when discussing herself, her business, and why she keeps on keeping on NO MATTER WHAT!

MizCEO: Who is Nakita Whittaker at her core?
Nakita: Im a business woman, lupus survivor and mother who inspires others, while working on myself, who learned long ago, you are never too young to build an empire and never too old to start a new dream.

MizCEO: Why are you so passionate about helping others; especially women?
Nakita: feel my ministry from God is women empowerment. I live for women realizing their worth and demanding the respect they deserve. In an era where the integrity of women rights is being questioned, we must understand now more than ever, when we invest in ourselves we go further.

MizCEO: Tell us about your businesses?
Nakita: Lanique Virtual Solutions (LVS) is a call center dedicated to providing work from home opportunities to mothers and women with chronic illnesses as inbound call center agents, handling calls for our Fortune 500 Companies.

MizCEO: What's next for Nakita personally?
Nakita: I'm in the process of writing another collaboration book titled Women Thriving Fearlessly in Business lead by publisher Erika Gilchrist. WTF in Business is set to be released in March of 2018.

MizCEO: What advice would you give to that person who's business is no doing so great and wants to give up?
Nakita: I would tell them to remember, if you don't go after what you want, you'll never have it. If you don't ask, the answer will always be no. If you don't step forward, you'll always stay in the sameplace.

Connect with Nakita:
Facebook: Nakita Whitaker

By Shirlonda Taylor

CREDIT IS KING

Many years ago, the Baby Boomer generation often used the saying, "Cash is King". Many people of that generation as well as generations prior, believed and lived their life by this rule. People would pay cash for good and services and would often declare if they couldn't pay cash, they didn't need it. Times have changed and there is a new Sheriff in town and his name is CREDIT!!

Credit and What it Means to You
Having a good credit rating (score) is very important and can stand between you and some major goals you may have set for yourself. Credit scores allows lenders to asses risk when issuing loans and when issuing lines of credit. Of course the lower the score the higher the risk. Low credit
scores translate into higher interest rates, higher insurance premiums and spending more money over a period of time. Often times a low score yields a flat out denial. Whereas, the higher the score the lower the risk which translates into lower rates which can saves hundreds and sometimes thousands of dollars over a period of time. Unfortunately 50% of Americans have a FICO Score (Fair Issac Corporation) that is considered to be poor. Let discuss the difference between your credit report and your credit report.

Credit Report vs. Credit Score: What's the Difference?
Credit Report
What is it? Your credit report is a reference to your records of credit history that you have built up over time.
Credit Score
Your credit score is a risk formula that uses the credit report to determine your creditworthiness.

Be sure to obtain a copy of your credit score annually. There are a number of credit tracking methods to stay on top of your credit score and activity taking place on your
credit profile.

To obtain a free copy of your credit report go to freeannualcreditreport.com Review your credit report for any errors or inaccuracies. Select a credit monitoring site/app to monitor credit movement on a regular basis.

If you are looking to raise your credit score keep the following tips and tricks in mind and
watch your credit score soar to the next level.

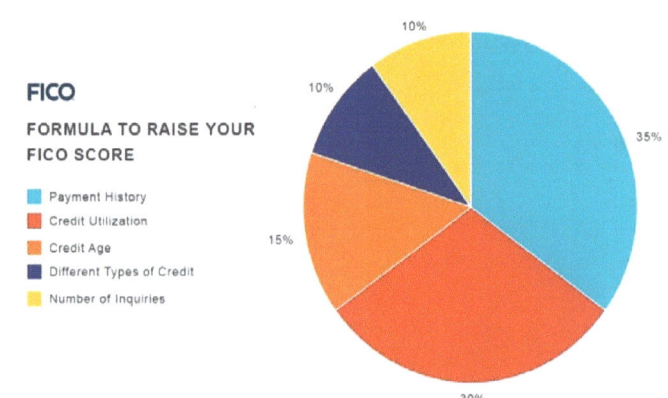

- Be sure to keep all revolving credit cards at 30% of credit limit.
- Contact the credit bureau and update all personal information. Deleting any aliases, old
addresses and employers. It is a good idea to remove any phone #'s
- Limited credit profile consider a Self-Lender Loan or become an authorized user on a
family members existing account. This is great idea for teenagers looking to start building
credit profile.
- Negotiate pay to delete for old collections if need be (this can sometimes decrease score
before benefiting score.)
- Consolidate student loan debt

If you are looking to purchase a home or increase your credit score, follow me on Facebook at Credit Movers....Change Your Credit Chance Your Life. Your credit score is your adult report card! What's your grade? Want to make your dreams and visions a lot more obtainable. If you change your credit, you truly can change your life.

Shirlonda Taylor is a 15 yr licensed loan originator for one of the top banks in the US She is passionate about financial literacy and assisting people live their best financial life (pie chart obtained from credit sesame)

TIESHENA DAVIS

It's Always about Potential

By Dr. Leslie Hodge

Dream it. Believe it. Become it. What happens when you have the audacity to believe in your childhood dreams…you become Tieshena Davis, multi-award-wining entrepreneur and CEO of Purposely Created Publishing.

With a passion for teaching, Tieshena always thought her students would be found in a school classroom. However, Tieshena has taken her passion and paired it with her calling and created a firm that teaches entrepreneurs, authors, and aspiring writers how to distinctively craft their experience, knowledge and expertise to share with the world.

In 2013, Tieshena encountered her true calling when she collaborated with 14 other women, to author and publish her first bestselling book - Surviving Shocking Situations: Finding Courage To Succeed In Spite of Life's Painful Moments. It was through that book writing and publishing experience that Tieshena realized and embraced her true life calling – to help others realize their potential. From publishing their stories to turning their message into a mission, creating a course from life experiences, launching speaking careers and teaching entrepreneurs how to monetize their gifts in writing, are just a few ways Tieshena helps others reach their full potential, and establish more credibility, visibility and profitability.

With 97% of her clients being entrepreneurs, and because many of them want to be established as a subject specialist, expert or authority in their field, Tieshena believes success begins with clarity and having the end result in mind.

Tieshena infuses her 20 years of strategic management and organizational leadership experience, with the expertise of her 22-member publishing professionals team. Collectively through brand assessment, literary editing, design

TIESHENA DAVIS

aesthetics, layout formatting, presale planning and post release review, each client is supported and positioned for success. When it comes to branding, the biggest mistake is one word...clarity. Failure identifying your target audience, their challenges, needs or desires, and being able to answer why they should look to you as the expert or authority on a specific topic, is what keeps one from attaining their professional and financial goals. Tieshena believes branding is a promise delivered—it's the perception you create, which is measured by what you say you will do and consistently deliver. If you think you have established a brand, ask yourself, "What do people think, feel or say when I am not in the room? Does it align with what I promised? Did I deliver?". If you can answer yes, then you know you have begun the process of developing a reliable and notable brand.

One clear message is Purposely Created Publishing...Creating Distinctive Books with Intentional Results, is not only a publishing company where you can publish literary works that promotes social awareness, education and personal transformation, but it is also where you will be celebrated.

In 2016, Tieshena created and executive produced the inaugural ceremony of The Indie Author Legacy Awards. Sponsored by Black Enterprise, this annual event not only celebrates independent authors, but it also serves as an opportunity to honor impact-centered writers who serve as unsung heroes within our communities. Through teaching, publishing and celebrating authors, Tieshena Davis is helping others realize and reach their fullest potential. Her legacy will continuously live on through the 360 books published and brands she has already established. What's next for the publishing house expert Tieshena Davis? The answer is FILM. It's time to take independent authors and their literary works to the big screen to create another opportunity for them to impact lives using a different form of media.

Stay Connected with Tieshena Davis:
FB: /publishyourgift
IG: @asktiedavis&@publishyourgift
Website: www.asktiedavis.com & www.publishyourgift.com

*Submitted by
Dr. Leslie Hodge, founder and operator of Scripts & Beyond, LLC - a medication review and consulting company, is a registered pharmacist and has a passion for people understanding their medications and improving their health. Connect with Dr. Hodge on FB @scriptsandbeyond, IG@dr.hodge or www.drlesliehodge.com.*

HEALTH & WELLNESS - MEET RENEE WATTS

RENEE WATTS

By Santisha Walker

Alright ladies, let's talk hair! What woman doesn't desire a head full of healthy hair? Whether you choose to rock your hair short, mid-length or down your back, I'm sure you long for healthy, full hair. When most of us think about healthy hair, we consider the actual hair strand. However, after an intriguing conversation with Renee Watts, a gifted hair stylist, owner of Believe Salon & Believe Hair Solutions, and Certified Hair Practitioner, I learned the importance of focusing on our internal health to produce healthy hair. This is a vital subject matter amongst women in today's society, and Renee strives to bring clarity to this popular topic.

Renee, what attracted you to the hair styling profession?
RW: Years ago, when I searched for hair stylists for my own hair, I was frustrated because the stylists didn't provide what I was in search of. I would often have to instruct them on how to style my hair, and after doing so the styles wouldn't last long. In addition, I was spending a lot of money on stylists. Also, there were times when my hair began falling out. So, I decided I needed to go to school for hair. I was not sure how it was going to work out, but once I began attending I knew I found my niche! There was an immediate connection! Years later I realized that the hair styling profession is not just about "styling hair", but more about contributing to a woman's confidence. I came to this realization as I styled inmates hair while working at a juvenile youth facility. Many of these young ladies had damaged hair due to stress and life circumstances, and I was able to enhance their self-esteem by caring for their hair.

So, would you say hair styling is like a ministry for you?
RW: Yes, most definitely. It's like when you go to church in a broken state and you know you need

HEALTH & WELLNESS - MEET RENEE WATTS

something to give you a boost. When clients sit in my chair I know my purpose is to provide care for their hair in a way that they leave confident, knowing their hair is one less thing to worry about.

You are now focusing more on hair health & wellness. Why has your focus now shifted to this specialty?

RW: My shift actually started in the juvenile youth facility, but I did not realize it. Then, when I moved to North Carolina from New Jersey, I was gaining older clientele whose struggle was hair loss. So, I had to learn to make the connection between hair loss and its causes. I used to focus on styling hair but being that my clientele did not have much hair and the hair they had was unhealthy, I had to study how to properly care for, treat and grow hair first before I could style the hair. Currently, I am in another transition phase due to the need to teach women about the importance of taking care of themselves internally in order to produce healthy strands of hair. It's not about the length of the hair that makes it healthy because some women don't desire long hair, but the focus is on what goes on the inside of the body and scalp to contribute to your body's ability to grow healthy hair.

Where do you envision yourself as a Hair Practitioner in the future as the hair industry continues to change?

RW: I see myself shifting into teaching and educating stylists, as well as our community. Last year I decided to adjust my lifestyle after battling with severe iron deficiency leading to continuous iron and blood transfusions, and since making the necessary changes my own hair and skin have improved. I actually haven't had to go to the doctor since making these changes. To continue on my path of hair health & wellness, I desire to complete my current trichology program. I also plan to use my hair practitioner certification and non-surgical hair replacement certification to partner with health specialists and practitioners to teach others the importance of their personal choices and the affect it has on not only their hair, skin and outer appearance, but their entire being!

Do you receive any push back from your clientele, particularly black women when you take an internal lifestyle approach to their hair care versus simply styling the hair strands?

For the most part, my clientele has been receptive to my shift in hair care. The most challenging part is the lifestyle changes, particularly when it comes to eating habits. The clients who have embraced my approach to caring for their hair have seen rewarding results and they love them! I teach my clients that using products focused on making hair strands appear beautiful on underlying unhealthy hair is like using band-aids on a bleeding wound. Several band-aids may cover the wound, but they won't stop the bleeding.

HEALTH & WELLNESS - MEET RENEE WATTS

WHAT WOULD YOU SAY ARE THE TOP 3 ESSENTIAL TIPS FOR GREAT HAIR CARE?

- Go to your doctor and have your bloodwork checked. Bloodwork should include your iron level, full thyroid panel, Vitamin D, B-complex vitamins, and hormone levels. These are components of a hair strand that are needed to contribute to healthy hair.

- Incorporate dark green vegetables into your diet, and if possible, take a break from meat to help detox your gut. Also, include fiber into your diet to contribute to gut health.

- Try to stay away from continual protective styling. At most use a protective style once weekly and leave it in the entire week. This will reduce the amount of strain on the scalp.

How can readers connect with you?
You can visit my website at www.believehairsolutions.com. There you will find a link for a consultation. I am also on Facebook and Instagram @believehairsolution.

About the Author: Santisha Walker is a Registered Nurse, Certified Wellness Coach, Entrepreneur, Author, Speaker, and Nurse Branding Coach. She has an immense passion of empowering others to live their best life through total wellness and balanced living. She is a devoted wife to her loving and supportive husband, and appreciations spending time with those she holds dear to her heart. You can connect with Santisha through her boutique consulting company, Walker Group Health & Wellness at walkergrouphw.com, through her personal site at SantishaWalker.com, or through her Facebook and Instagram pages @santishawalkerrn.

BLACK GIRLS HEAR BY MIZCEO STAFF

BLACK GIRLS HEAR:
Untold Stories of the Marginalized, Unsafe & Unwelcomed

Is there anything you find particularly challenging about writing or coming up with a concept for your book?
As a publisher, I focus on self-help books that empower women and the community. As an author, I usually lead with topics that I am passionate about. I find that passion compels me to complete any project I endeavor. With the Black Girls Hear Anthology, I knew I wanted to rally the stories of many women to gain and offer varying perspectives of our experiences—both collective and individual—to the world. This was challenging in that communication became a necessary medium I never had to use in my solo projects. However, I couldn't be prouder of how we all came together to create this work that is impacting women around the globe.

What was the hardest part of completing this project?
Well, the aim of Black Girls Hear was to bring together a collective of women's experiences and stories with the hopes of giving young women a glimpse into our worlds that they may find themselves in our stories; or even that they may be able to relate to and be empowered to articulate a phenomenon they are already encountering. But, truth be told, the hardest part for we authors was giving ourselves permission to release our stories in the first place. Often, we (black women) hold in our pain in an effort to protect our dignity.

What is the mission you set out to accomplish with your voice in this book?

BLACK GIRLS HEAR BY MIZCEO STAFF

Black Girls Hear was written for every black woman and girl who's racial and gender identity has made her doubt her abilities; for every black woman and girl who's ever experienced being judged or punished more harshly for the identical infractions by a white counterpart; for every black woman and girl who's been told she's too aggressive, too loud, too sassy; for every black woman and girl who's had an experience where someone did not expect her to be smart or capable.

It was written to expose our narrative and to illuminate just how gender and race, and their intersection, influence how black women and girls are treated in society; how black women are often ignored in policy discussions. It was written to give voice to stories and perspectives that help shed light on gender injustice and societal bias.

What were the literary, psychological and/or logistical challenges in bringing Black Girls Hear to life?
I've written lots of books over the past six years. However, in the case of Black Girls Hear, we had to be really vulnerable. Vulnerable enough to share experiences that hurt us to our core. My co-Authors—Jessica Mosley, Audria Richmond, Lucie Matsouaka, Keemia H. Shaw and Lesleigh Muasi—all had to dig deep and ask ourselves what we were willing to give of ourselves to help women thrive and heal. So yes, some of it was psychological. I talked about my experiences with name shaming in childhood and adulthood. Lucie talked about her experience as an immigrant new to this country (USA). Another author, Audria Richmond, discusses awkwardness as a black female in the digital space. So, there are some raw, lived experiences that readers have access to. And once it's out there, it's out there. Everyone's process for writing is different. Explain yours. When writing, I usually write in blocks of time. It helps me to get a lot done in chunks of allotted time frames. In fact, my most popular book to date, was written in two days. Generally, I begin with the end in mind. So, I write the conclusion first and then work backwards. (The intro is the very last thing I complete.) I then create 8-10 themes or chapters. From there it's just a matter of fleshing out the content and thinking through the accoutrements such as quotes, passages, statistics, etc.

What books are you currently reading? Why this author?
I am currently reading The Hollywood Commandments by DeVon Franklin, #GIRLBOSS by Sophia Amoruso, and Exponential Living by Sheri Riley. I tend to read authors I can relate to, be it their business trajectory, their speaking or their general vibes. I vibe with each of these authors and respect their perspectives. Additionally, I read all research by Kimberlé Crenshaw, an American civil rights advocate and a leading scholar of critical race theory. She is a full-time professor at the UCLA School of Law and Columbia Law School, where she specializes in race and gender issues. Her work inspired me to embark upon the Black Girls Hear project and seek co-authors and contributors to bring it to life.

What new authors have piqued your interest?
My interest is especially piqued by these two authors lately: New author, Michael A. Strickland who recently released a book called Penetrating Thoughts. It teaches transformative thinking and meditation. Because our thought life dictates our lives, this book is a page-turner. Also, Author Letonia Page and her book A Thousand Wishes. It delves into relationships and the signs of co-dependence, with themes all women can relate to. It's deep!

What advice would you give other writers?
I run a self-publishing company, Literacy Moguls, and I am often asked this question. My advice to authors with platforms is to write about what you are an expert in. Think about what people ask you the most and then give them what they want. Listening is key. You would be surprised at how much what you know will set you apart.

A great book has what?
A lesson to be learned a curiosity to be piqued.

Wisdom Series Journals

$5.00 + Tax

Trust Journal

"Trusting God means more when you stop trying to help him"

Faith Journal

Faith: the witness that causes you to believe no matter what

- 42 pages
- Poetry
- Testimonies
- Space to write

These journals offer a place to write it out, while allowing God to work it out.

If Interested, go to: bit.ly/JournalForm
Use Coupon Code: JAM10

JamBugg Creative Spreading & Company

INTRODUCING LILLIE MAE CONT'D

MizCEO: What advice would you give your younger self about growing up as a woman in this world?
Lillie Mae: In a world that will try to convince you that you are too much or not enough, remember that being your authentic self is always just right!

MizCEO: If you were the first woman president, what would be your first order of business?
Lillie Mae: I grew up in a very underserved community, so my first order of business would be establishing success ambassadors; in similar communities around the country. These ambassadors would introduce children early-on to the financial, technological and entrepreneurial insights that will enhance their aptitude for success as adults.

Make sure to keep up with Lillie Mae for event updates, business tips and other entrepreneur opportunities, be sure to connect with me on Instagram @GlambitiousIAm

THE MizCEO ENTREPRENEURIAL BRAND

What we offer:

Book/Magazine Publishing

Public Relations Services

Radio

Life/Business Coaching Services

MISTERCEO OF THE MONTH JAMIE MCGRONE

MISTERCEO

I think the reason why I have been successful in my field of work is because I am humble and I always left Room to grow.

Jamie McGrone is a man of compassion and love, a man who strongly believes in God and a father of 2 beautiful children. He is a man with many different gifts that God gave him and he is a man who wants to see the world happy. He is a man who believes in giving back and helping others find their purpose and destiny

MizCEO: How long have you been in business?
JM: I have been in business for more than 20+ years

MizCEO: Why did you pick this particular field to do business in?
JM: I picked the field of work that I am in because it allowed me to be mobile and spend more time with both my children

MizCEO: Tell us about a challenge you have had in business and how you have overcome it?
JM: The challenge I had in business was relocating because it took me out of my comfort zone but one thing I found was that it pushed me to refocus myself, think bigger and become a better businessman

MizCEO: Why do you feel you have been as successful as you have in your business?

JM: I think the reason why I have been successful in my field of work is because I am humble and I always left Room to grow. I understand that without The people, I would not be in business, so I quickly learned that when You treat others with respect, You get It back and that is The growth of a man

MizCEO: Why are you so compelled on seeing other men win BIG?
JM: I am so compelled to see men win because It is all about leadership. It's about motivating and inspiring The younger generation and showing compassion so that they to may lead. It's about being in position to live your most amazing life and living It to The fulllest

MizCEO: Fun fact about yourself.
JM: I would like to think I am a joker because I love to see people laugh. I love to see people happy, so I aim to please

MizCEO: How can we stay connected with you? (Social media handles)
Instagram: @jmcgrone
Facebook: Jamie McGrone
Twitter: @jamiethewriter

WHY IS EVERYONE RAVING ABOUT DELISA NEWWILLIAMS

By: DeLisa New Williams

A Pregnant BOSS GUIDE:
HOW TO BEAT THE HEAT AND STILL SEAL THE DEAL

It happened to be right at the end of spring, early summer and here I was in my second trimester working through the pressures of writing my books and increased orders within my t-shirt business The Hem of His Garment Custom Apparel. My third published book, No Longer Am I A Baby Mama just had a successful launch and even though I was nurturing this life growing inside of me, I was quickly booked for readings, speaking engagements, and panel discussions. Events are great, aside from accepting the fact that your body is changing rapidly and clothes don't quite fit the same anymore hence forcing you to constantly shop for this new round figure. However, imagine running a business, being pregnant, and feeling like 200 degrees fahrenheit everyday baking in the summer heat. It was these imperative moments where I realized being a CEO and a mother-to-be in the summertime was more than I'd bargained for. It was one thing being a pregnant entrepreneur, but it was another thing doing it all while trying to beat the summer heat. Something had to happen and happen fast. I love my business and the life growing inside of my belly, but I didn't want to sabotage everything I've worked for because of influx of hormones, burning sweats, mood swings, irritation, along with some aches and pains which could result in me waking up one day and saying, "Forget it ALL!"

WHY IS EVERYONE RAVING ABOUT DELISA NEWWILLIAMS

There's no secret that pregnant women's hormones are heightened and the summer can be the most miserable time for any mother-to-be. So just how does the "expecting" CEO manage the growing business and belly, yet still enjoy the beautiful weather? Here are a some tips that are a sure way to keep your business on your client's radar and provide you with some memories that aren't all bad. Hopefully it won't have you sharing stories with your family and friends deeming it to be "thee worst summer ever".

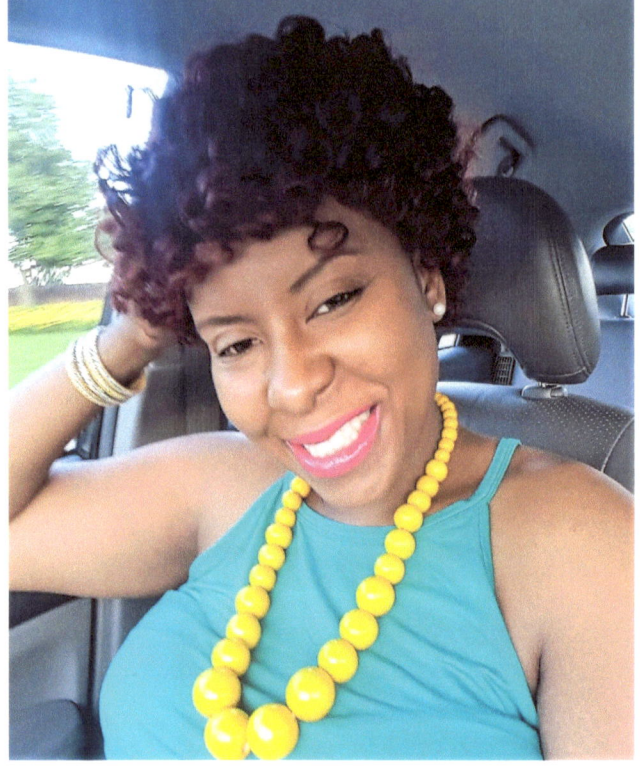

Tip One - Forgetfulness. Your brain is working overtime and you might be experiencing this diagnosis pregnancy brain; where it seems you tend to forget everything...even the simplest things. I took some time and had a chance to chat with Ariel Howard-White, a Mompreneur Strategist of *Boss Mom Life* who's currently carrying her 2nd child and in her 3rd trimester and asked what tips does she use to help overcome pregnancy brain and get those tasks completed for her business. "(This pregnancy) has not only zapped all of my brain cells, but my energy as well. Normally I set 3-4 goals I want to achieve daily...I've learned that I must listen to my body and adjust things...so instead I set 1 goal a day that I must hit (and stopped) trying to balance everything." Ariel mentioned, "My tip is to focus on prioritizing what matters most in (this) season, I promise your business will not suffer for it."

Tip Two - Stay hydrated. You can't focus on making any crucial deals in your business with headaches and swollen feet from dehydration. So remember to always, yes always...drink plenty of fluids. It not only helps cool you down, but the refreshing taste of a cool beverage will keep you right on track with getting your job done.

Tip Three - Be okay with taking breaks. This is a perfect time to learn how to successfully delegate tasks to others so the business can still operate while you're nurturing the seed growing inside of you. Walk away from your business and enjoy the great outdoors, go see this week's feature film, or indulge in a sweet treat at your local ice cream shoppe. Either way, your business will be handled and when you decide to return from your break, you'll be well rested.

Tip Four - Video conference meetings. We know sometimes putting on clothes, getting all dolled up, and hopping in the car for a meeting can be a chore. Therefore, instead of cancelling meetings all together opt for a video conference that way you can still meet with your customer, enjoy some A/C, and relax with your feet elevated to avoid pregnancy swollen feet and ankles. Your clients will never be able to tell the difference.

Tip Five - Pregnancy Exercise. Swimming is a sure way to stay cool during the summer and it's a great form of exercise. Walking is too! Exercise releases endorphins which triggers a positive feeling in your body preparing you to enjoy and seize the day.

Tip Six - Pose for the frame. Hey let's be honest depending on your business, your customers are used to seeing you in the public eye. So give them a picture, video, or even do a live every now and again to let them know you're still working and enjoying your pregnancy. When your customers see you enjoying life, having fun in the sun (or beach), and happy they'll respond better with sending more business your way. This is not the time to go into hiding. The last thing you want is for your customers to think you're no longer working because you're pregnant.

Remember, your customers purchase from you because they like you. It's not all about what you're selling!

DeLisa NewWilliams (@delisanewwilliams), a contributing writer for MizCEO magazine, is a published author, cutting-edge speaker, wife, and mother living in Chicago.

HEALTH & WELLNESS MATTERS: WOMEN MAKING IT HAPPEN

By Jacqueline Miller

CINDY PEAY

OWNER AND CREATOR OF A PEACE OF ME SKINCARE
Harlem, NY USA

How long have you been in the business of health & wellness?
While I have been actively involved in health & wellness initiatives for several years, I've officially been in business since March of 2018.

How did you decide upon your company's name, A Peace of Me (APOM)?
I was seeking inner-peace within myself, and once I found it, I started on a journey of healing. I subsequently wanted to share a piece of my discoveries and new lifestyle with others who were seeking the same transformation.

Why did you select this particular field to do business in?
I selected this field because there are so many skin care companies that sell beauty products. I wanted to offer skincare products that have healing properties for your mind, body, and spirit. I believe if your temple (body) is at peace, then you will always feel beautiful, inside and out.

What makes you and your business different from other similar businesses?
Today's skincare companies are feeding into women's insecurities about how they look, and often neglecting to focus on how they feel. At A

HEALTH & WELLNESS MATTERS: WOMEN MAKING IT HAPPEN

Peace of Me Skincare, we focus on creating skin and self-care products to beautify the mind, body, and spirit. We use organic essential oils with uplifting and healing properties to help calm skin due to emotional stress. We also care about your welling being. We grow herbs and flowers in our garden to create botanical tools to assist in your self-care rituals, such as meditations, yoga sessions, and prayers. We realize that healing comes in a variety of forms; however, our focus is on the creation of natural products to help assist you with the healing or maintenance of your entire well-being.

What has been the GREATEST challenge (nearly made you want to give up) that you have faced since starting in this business and how you have overcome it?
One day I was applying for a pop-up market and realized I was moving faster than my resources would allow. I had already tapped into my savings and didn't want to take a loan of any kind. I stepped away from creating and sat down with my family, and we came up with a financial plan that helped me spend less so I could put more money into my business. I'm grateful that I spoke up when I was in need because I was ready to throw in the towel. I'm most grateful that the person who stepped forward first to offer support was my loving husband. It pays to have your partner in your corner when you are pursuing your dreams.

What would you say are the greatest obstacles to women maintaining and focusing on good health and how does your business provide a solution?
Women wear many hats. We are mothers, wives, caretakers, and so much more. We're so busy taking care of others that we forget to take time for ourselves. At APOM, we like to remind women that it's perfectly ok to take an hour or two for themselves. Our company provides organic products with calming and healing ingredients to relieve stress and find clarity. We also encourage taking a few minutes to meditate each day, so we offer floral smudge sticks and floral wands to assist in your self- care routines.

What advice would you offer another woman beginning her entrepreneurial journey?
Write your business plan down and do your research. When I started my business I didn't follow my plan and was in a rush to get the company up and running. In doing this, I overlooked important marketing and financial plans that cost me time and money. Trusting the process is essential.

What three health & wellness words of wisdom or tips do you have for women in 2018?
Always strive to be a better version of yourself. Never say that you can't do something. Instead, choose to take a break and revisit the task or issue at a later time. I believe in the power of affirmations and mantras, and I recite this one every day, "SPEAK IT, BELIEVE IT AND RECEIVE IT."

For more information about Cindy Peay, visit her website: www.apeaceofmeskincare.com
Follow her on Instagram: @apeaceofmeskincare

Jacqueline Miller is an international bestselling author, speaker, and certified life coach. She's an expert in empowering high-achieving women to excel in their lives. Her programs provide strategies and resources to obtain clarity, as well as techniques to successfully manage their careers, family obligations, relationships, finances, time management, and self-care. In addition, she is a trainer and consultant for leading edge corporate clients. Stay connected with Jacqueline Miller by following her on social media. Facebook, Instagram and Twitter @mogulmomdujour as well as on LinkedIn: thejacquelinemiller. Visit her website www. jacquelinedujour.com

MIZCEO FEATURE OF THE MONTH: NICOLE MASON

THE RADICAL
NICOLE MASON

MizCEO: Why is Nicole Mason on a mission to help women #ShowUpGreat?

NM: I was so blessed to have a mother who instilled confidence in me from as early as I can remember in my life. She would always tell me, "Nicole, you don't ask for respect, you demand it. And, it's not about what you have on, it's about how you show up." I realized as I grew older that my mother was very intentional about fortifying me from the inside out, as opposed to allowing the world to dictate to me from the outside in on who or what I could be and accomplish. Confidence is a key ingredient to success in every area of a woman's life. Due to my mother's impartation in my life, I am on a mission to help women to embrace who they are unapologetically. In addition to my mother's influence in my life, my grandmother was and will forever be my shero! My grandmother had an 8th grade education, but she was a Boss before it was popular or acceptable for women to be entrepreneurs. Unlike women today who have a choice in becoming a business owner, my grandmother's trek into the world of business was for survival. She didn't have many choices at that time in history. My grandmother made many sacrifices for her family. I am very sensitive to those sacrifices and believe that I have an obligation to do everything that I do with a spirit of excellence. And the reality is, we all stand on the shoulders

Cont'd on next page

NAKITA WHITTAKER - THE SURVIVOR CONT'D

MizCEO: Tell us about your businesses?
Nakita: Lanique Virtual Solutions (LVS) is a call center dedicated to providing work from home opportunities to mothers and women with chronic illnesses as inbound call center agents, handling calls for our Fortune 500 Companies.

MizCEO: What's next for Nakita personally?
Nakita: I'm in the process of writing another collaboration book titled Women Thriving Fearlessly in Business lead by publisher Erika Gilchrist. WTF in Business is set to be released in March of 2018.

MizCEO: What advice would you give to that person who's business is no doing so great and wants to give up?
Nakita: I would tell them to remember, if you don't go after what you want, you'll never have it. If you don't ask, the answer will always be no. If you don't step forward, you'll always stay in the sameplace.

Connect with Nakita:
Facebook: Nakita Whitaker

MIZCEO FEATURE OF THE MONTH: NICOLE MASON

MizCEO: Why is Nicole Mason on a mission to help women #ShowUpGreat?

NM: I was so blessed to have a mother who instilled confidence in me from as early as I can remember in my life. She would always tell me, "Nicole, you don't ask for respect, you demand it. And, it's not about what you have on, it's about how you show up." I realized as I grew older that my mother was very intentional about fortifying me from the inside out, as opposed to allowing the world to dictate to me from the outside in on who or what I could be and accomplish. Confidence is a key ingredient to success in every area of a woman's life. Due to my mother's impartation in my life, I am on a mission to help women to embrace who they unapologetically. In addition to my mother's influence in my life, my grandmother was and will forever be my shero! My grandmother had an 8 th grade education, but she was a Boss before it was popular or acceptable for women to be entrepreneurs. Unlike women today who have a choice in becoming a business owner, my grandmother's trek into the world of business was for survival. She didn't have many choices at that time in history. My grandmother made many sacrifices for her family. I am very sensitive to those sacrifices and believe that I have an obligation to do everything that I do with a spirit of excellence. And the reality is, we all stand on the shoulders of women who have walked many paths for us to do what we do and to be who we are today. We all have an obligation to #ShowUpGreat!

MizCEO: Why is Nicole Mason on a mission to help women #ShowUpGreat?

NM: I was so blessed to have a mother who instilled confidence in me from as early as I can remember in my life. She would always tell me, "Nicole, you don't ask for respect, you demand it. And, it's not about what you have on, it's about how you show up." I realized as I grew older that my mother was very intentional about fortifying me from the inside out, as opposed to allowing the world to dictate to me from the outside in on who or what I could be and accomplish. Confidence is a key ingredient to success in every area of a woman's life. Due to my mother's impartation in my life, I am on a mission to help women to embrace who they unapologetically. In addition to my mother's influence in my life, my grandmother was and will forever be my shero! My grandmother had an 8 th grade education, but she was a Boss before it was popular or acceptable for women to be entrepreneurs. Unlike women today who have a choice in becoming a business owner, my grandmother's trek into the world of business was for survival. She didn't have many choices at that time in history. My grandmother made many sacrifices for her family. I am very sensitive to those sacrifices and believe that I have an obligation to do everything that I do with a spirit of excellence. And the reality is, we all stand on the shoulders of women who have walked many paths for us to do what we do and to be who we are today. We all have an obligation to #ShowUpGreat!

MizCEO: How long have you been in the Leadership Coaching sector? Why Leadership Coaching?

NM: I officially received my Leadership Coaching Certificate from Georgetown University in 2011. However, I have been coaching leaders for many years. I am a preacher and have been honored to serve women since 1998 by coaching and mentoring, but the word coaching was not necessarily the title used to describe the interactions. Although coaching has been around for a long time, the concept is overused today. Unfortunately, there are many people who call themselves coaches but lack the credentials to support the title. There is an art and science to coaching and people should not enter a coaching relationship haphazardly. I know of many people who have hired a "coach" without getting the desired results. From my vantage point, a coach should not only have coaching education but should have also been the recipient of coaching with transformational results before coaching others. I chose Leadership Coaching, because I serve as Coach and Confidante to leaders in ministry and the marketplace. I didn't set out to be a "Leader's Leader." I believe that God endowed me with wisdom and truth that leaders are drawn to and have experienced over the years. I have coached senior level executives who have referred their colleagues to me. The one thing that they know for sure is that I will be honest, truthful and confidential. It is my honor and privilege to serve those that are leading

MIZCEO FEATURE OF THE MONTH: NICOLE MASON

others. Leaders need a safe and sacred space to be vulnerable and to get good, Godly wisdom. Although I have coaching education to support my title of coach, the anointing on my life is a tremendous bonus for every woman that hires me as her coach.

MizCEO: What can people expect from you in this 2 nd quarter of 2018?
NM: I am excited about my very first book collaboration that will be launching in June. The book is about Faith, and the Co-Authors are first time authors. I know that many people want to write a book but don't always know where to start. I offered this opportunity to build the momentum for the women to write their own books. I have provided training and coaching throughout the process. I also have some amazing Celebrity Co-Authors who have partnered with me to share their stories of how faith helped them to overcome an obstacle in their lives. I am excited about the impact that this book will have on the world for generations to come.

MizCEO: It's been stated that success is intentional. What is that one intentional thing you do everyday to ensure your success in business?
NM: I pray about everything, so it is important to me to stay connected to my source. God is my source. In addition to prayer, I am intentional about ensuring that everything that I do is directly connected to my purpose of helping women to be who they are authentically and creating success on their own terms.

MizCEO: What is success to you?
NM: Success is doing what I know I am called to do in the earth and making impact in the lives of others. The way that this is implemented in my life is through the establishment of goals and taking the necessary actions each day to accomplish those goals. Finally, success to me is acknowledging my own greatness and saluting the greatness in others.

www.facebook.com/nicolesherronmason • www.twitter.com/nicolesmason
www.instagram.com/nicolesmason

CHERYL PEAVY - COVER STORY

Why is everyone talking about Cheryl Peavy?

WHY is everyone talking about Cheryl Peavy? Is it because she is one gifted sister! From writing for national media outlets, to interviewing high achieving men and women, to publishing books, is there any thing that this media giant can't do? Well listen in as we discuss with her The Art of Media.

Miz CEO: What inspired you to wrote your first book?
CP: What inspired me was that importance of bringing awareness to people pleasing. This is one topic that I rarely see discussed. There are so many people who live their lives for love, and acceptance. I used to be a people pleaser and by living my life for others, I lost my identity and lost so many precious years of being happy.

Miz CEO: Do you have a specific writing style?
CP: My writing style is narrative. I feel that most people need encouragement in their lives. Often times we look for stories to read of what we are experiencing. To get answers and to know that there is hope and we are not alone with some of the things that we go through.

Miz CEO: What books have most impacted your life (or life as an author)?
CP: The books that impact my life are stories of challenges and triumphs. I love to read others personal experiences. It helps me learn and grow as a person. It encourages me and inspires me so.

CHERYL PEAVY - COVER STORY

Miz CEO: What books are you currently reading? Why this author?
CP: I have been reading Becky A Davis book called 40 Days of Prayer for my Business. Marshawn Evans Daniels Believe Bigger. The reason I am reading these books because I want to stay encouraged and focus walking in my purpose. These two books do just that. When you are walking in your purpose you have to stay in constant prayer and having faith.

Miz CEO: If you had to do it all over again, would you change anything about your latest work?
CP: I would never change anything with my latest work. Everything that you do is a learning experience whether things go smoothly or not. You can never stop learning or growing.

Miz CEO: Is there anything you find particularly challenging about writing or coming up with a concept for your book?
CP: What I find most challenging is when you come up with your next writing project is not giving up. We can be our own worst critics. Negative thoughts come creeping up. Then you have to learn to fight those thoughts and keep pushing and following through with your idea.

Miz CEO: What was the hardest part of completing this project?
CP: The hardest part in completing this project was bringing my ideas to life. There was a lot of delays. When you have ideas and you want to bring it to life; sharing what your ideas are and having someone bring it to life was challenging. Eventually it all fell into place.

Miz CEO: What advice would you give other writers?
CP: My advice is to never give up. Your story matters! It is important to remember that what your story is that someone needs to hear it. If you touch one person, it's worth it!

Miz CEO: Describe the process in getting published?
CP: I have to say I had no idea what happens on the publishing end. I was shocked to learn all that goes into it. It takes time to make a project top notch. You have to trust the publisher and what they say would work better. From formatting, to graphics, to editing. All of it works together and I learn everything doesn't come together overnight. I have so much respect for publishers.

Miz CEO: Everyone's process for writing is different. Explain yours.
CP: Sharing from the heart. Being open and real with what you want to share. Others can related to reading books when they feel as though then can put themselves in another person's shoes. I want readers to feel like they are watching a movie as they are reading.

Miz CEO: What are 5 of your favorite books and why?
CP: My favorite books are the Bible, What I Know For Sure- Oprah Winfrey, To Kill A Mockingbird by Harper Lee, Command Your Morning by Dr. Cindy Trimm and Diary Of A People Pleaser compiled by Cheryl Peavy. I love these books because they drew me in. The bible

CHERYL PEAVY - COVER STORY

helps me get through life, while e Oprah's book inspired me and to Kill A Mockingbird was so well written that I couldn't put it down. Dr. Cindy Trimm drew me in to understand that I can command how my days go. Then Diary of A People Pleaser because it was my first compilation and it was a great book speaking on a Pleasing Others and how one can lose their identity and blessings by living to please others. I love the awareness it has brought to others.

Miz CEO: Please provide 3 "good to know" fact about you. Be creative. Tell us about your first job or the inspiration behind your writing.
CP: My first job was working at Sears. I was 19 and I was so happy to finally have my own money. My favorite food is McDonalds French Fries. What inspired me to start writing was when my mother passed away. I remember here always saying you are never too old to go after your dreams. I always loved writing growing up but was too afraid to do it.

Miz CEO: What is the mission you set out to accomplish with your voice in this book?
CP: My mission is make others stop and ask themselves this question. Am I living my life for me or living my life to please others? To understand the importance of being authentic and who you are! If people can't accept you for who you are, then you don't need them. I lived my life for so many years people pleasing and there is no rewards when you do so.

Miz CEO: Who are the authors you reread and why?
CP: Oprah Winfrey, Priscilla Shirer and Dr. Cindy Trimm. Just to name a few. Because I believe in reading things that draw you in over and over. There are many lessons that can be learned from one statement and a paragraph. I even write down things that make me have an aha moment from reading these authors over and over. Inspiration, motivation and encouragement is what they all add to my life.

Miz CEO: A great book has what?
CP: A great book in my opinion has your authenticity. When you are writing from a place of truth and your own voice, it speaks volumes.

Miz CEO: You develop character and ideas by....
CP: You develop character and ideas by the challenging experiences in your life. Those experiences grow you and take to you to the next level in life.

Miz CEO: Where would you travel if you could to write your next book?
CP: I would travel to Hawaii. The beautiful weather and beaches would be a great place for inspiration.

Miz CEO: What is the gift of reading and why does it around up a new world?
CP: It is an adventure. Not everybody in this world can read. I think a lot of people take reading for granted. Reading can open up new doors of living your dreams. You can get ideas for you next project. You can be encouraged, inspired and motivated to do things that you have always been afraid. Reading is powerful.

https://www.instagram.com/cherylpeavy/
https://twitter.com/cheryl_peavy
https://www.facebook.com/cheryl.peavy.3
https://m.facebook.com/CherylPeavyInnerLifeCoach/

www.ingramcontent.com/pod-product-compliance
Lightning Source LLC
Chambersburg PA
CBHW040452220526
45473CB00004B/1613